# Et Tú . . . Raza?

# Bilingual Press/Editorial Bilingüe

General Editor
    Gary D. Keller

Managing Editor
    Karen S. Van Hooft

Associate Editors
    Ann Waggoner Aken
    Theresa Hannon

Assistant Editor
    Linda St. George Thurston

Editorial Board
    Juan Goytisolo
    Francisco Jiménez
    Eduardo Rivera
    Mario Vargas Llosa


Address:
Bilingual Review/Press
Hispanic Research Center
Arizona State University
P.O. Box 872702
Tempe, Arizona 85287-2702
(602) 965-3867

# Et Tú . . . Raza?

alurista

Bilingual Press/Editorial Bilingüe
TEMPE, ARIZONA

ISBN 0-927534-48-7

Library of Congress Cataloging-in-Publication Data

Alurista.
    Et tú . . . Raza? / Alurista.
      p.   cm.
    English and Spanish.
    ISBN 0-927534-48-7 (paper)
    I. Title.
PS3551.L84E85    1994
811'.54—dc20                        94-34229
                                            CIP

*Cover design by Kerry Curtis*

*Front cover photo by Delilah Montoya*

*Back cover photo by Gloria González*

*Drawing on page viii by Zamná Urista*

Acknowledgments

Major new marketing initiatives have been made possible by the Lila Wallace-Reader's Digest Literary Publishers Marketing Development Program, funded through a grant to the Council of Literary Magazines and Presses.

Funding provided by a grant from the National Endowment for the Arts in Washington, D.C., a Federal agency.

# Contents

. . . in the beginning
was the Verb
            and the Verbo
    b
        struggle!
i . . . zaz!

**tango malvino**

PREGUNTA: señor secretario de agricultura, dado el presente estado tecnológicoindustREAL, ¿sería factible decir que los Estados Unidos pueden alimentar al mundo, acabar con el hambre?

SECRETARIO: well, well, well. el problema radica en la proliferación de los pueblos tercer mundistas. es necesario esterilizar a las naciones pobres como la India y latinoamérica.

(NOTICIAS): millones de galones de leche serán vaciados en el mar este año. este año miles de productores agrícolas recibirán subsidios para no cosechar. este año cientos de megatoneladas de queso terminarán en las cavernas. este año se limitará el número de tractores ensamblados. este año se reducirá la producción de comida en lata. este año se venderán más armas que comida.

UN INDIO: nuestros hijos son nuestros cebúes y nuestros tractores. una familia grande nos permite trabajar más tierras aun así nos falta buena semilla y abono. nuestros hijos son nuestro seguro social y nuestra televisión.

PREGUNTA: ¿pueden los Estados Unidos acabar con el hambre?

SECRETARIO: well, well, well.
hay que acabar con el comunismo. hay que

acabar con la superreproducción. hay que acabar con la ociosidad. hay que acabar con las guerrillas. hay que acabar con la sexualidad.

(NOTICIAS): millones mueren de hambre en el tercer mundo. la reforma agraria en américa latina aún sufre de parálisis. el maíz que se les da a las vacas norteamericanas podría alimentar al mundo entero. los perros comen mejor en los "estados" que cualquier ciudadano continental. el costo de un dirigible atómico pondría un tractor al alcance de cada ejido latinoamericano.

PREGUNTA: ¿pueden los Estados Unidos acabar con el hambre?

SECRETARIO: well, well, well.
el problema radica en la corrupción.
hay que acabar con la corrupción.
hay que acabar con las drogas.
hay que acabar con los insurgentes.
hay que acabar con los malos hábitos higiénicos.
hay que acabar con los vicios.
hay que acabar con la prostitución.

PREGUNTA: señor secretario. sin rodeos esta vez, por favor.
conteste sí o no.
¿pueden los Estados Unidos acabar con el hambre?

SECRETARIO: well, well, well.
as u all say in the South,
sí sinior, por supuesto. if the price is right!

2

RÓTULOS:      PRODUCCIÓN MILITAR NO ALIMENTICIA
GUERRA EN VENTA, EXTINGUIR EL SEXO
QUE COMAN BALAS, NO HABRÁ PAN

MEDITACIÓN:   ¿EXTERMINAR AL HAMBRE . . .
. . . O
. . . AL HOMBRE?

# lastango news

QUESTION: secretary of agriculture, sir. given the present technologicoindustREAL state . . . is it feasible for the United States of America to end hunger, to feed the world?

SECRETARY: WELL, WELL, WELL . . . the problem is rooted in the proliferation of third world people, it is necessary to sterilize poor nations such as those in Asia, Africa, and Latin America.

(NEWS): millions of gallons of milk will be emptied into the sea this year, this year thousands of agrifarms will receive subsidies in order *not* to farm, this year megatons of cheese will end up in the caves, this year the number of tractors assembled will be curtailed, this year the production of canned food will be reduced, this year more weapons will be sold than food.

A HINDU: our children are our zebus and our tractors. a large family allows us to till more land. even so we lack good seed and organic fertilizers. our children are our *tele* vision.

QUESTION: can the United States end world hunger?

SECRETARY: WELL, WELL, WELL . . .
we must end communism, put an end to overproduction, we must definitely end

4

"idleness," we must terminate guerrillas,
sex must be abolished.

(NEWS): millions die of hunger in the third world.
agrarian reform suffers, still, from paraly-
sis. the corn-fed northamerican cows
could nourish the entire planet. dogs eat
better in the U.S. of A. than any citizen in
the third world. the cost of a nuclear war-
head would put a tractor within the reach
and use of every Asian, African, and Latin
American small farm . . . diesel and all.

QUESTION: without beating around the bush this
time, secretary, sir, please answer the
question.

SECRETARY: WELL, WELL, WELL . . .
the problem is rooted in corruption.
we must terminate corruption!
we must terminate drug trafficking!
we must terminate insurgency!
we must terminate natality!
we must terminate, terminate, terminate!

QUESTION: once and for all! answer YES or NO!
can the United States end world hunger?!

SECRETARY: WELL, WELL, WELL . . .
well, of course, as they say in Latin
America
sí sinior! *if the price is right!*

SLOGANS: PRODUCE WEAPONS NOT FOOD
WAR ON SALE EXTINGUISH SEX
FEED THEM BULLETS THERE WILL BE NO
BREAD

5

MEDITATION: end hunger or terminate man?
liberty, community, and bread or bombs?
just us or justice?

## southwestern trek in four-part harmony

*first movement*

could i have a dollar?
the sun peeks
behind the cameras focusing
to capture those raisin, black sun
almond eyes and hustling grin
. . . an old man at the age of seven
dark clouds cloak the sky
i wear a saguayo mexican hat
little floyd asks then
if he can have my "stetson"
. . . "u can keep the feathers
. . . i got some myself"
our heads r roughly the same size
so r our feet
. . . "i'll trade it for your boots"
i say to him with a smirk
. . . "it's gonna drizzle tonight"
little floyd whittles out and
disappears on the dust of
his rebuilt huffy bike

*second movement*

. . . "oh, those wonderful, wonnnderful kids,"
one says with gleeful superficiality
"they remind me of my nephews"
—i bet your nephews
wouldn't come up to a stranger
and ask for a dollar
. . . "oh no, they wouldn't"
she snaps back with self-importance
—do u know why they wouldn't?
. . . "well, *they* were raised

7

by two schoolteachers"
—you're equivocating, i say to her
carefully and ironically enunciating
the sunday word i'm hurling
. . . "i beg your pardon!
—*they* wouldn't go up to a complete
stranger and ask for a dollar
because they have a dollar, or two . . ."
briskly she walks away clutching
her recently acquired squash blossom
sterling cast necklace to her heart
inside the pueblo mission a lecture awaits
myth is easier to handle than class

*third movement*

it wasn't hard to find my spot
a small clearing surrounded
by piñon trees glowed with
my colors, the hues were friendly
the dusk was more like ashes
than it was embers or the crack
between two worlds, the campfire
crackled with murmured voices
rain clouds hovered around
the zuni mountains' mesquite
rain trickled gently and warm
this evening, this very dew
exactly forty years after
the first A-bomb test
white sands remains a ghost
white house still posits
"limited nuclear warfare"
as a plausible "defense"
the piñon knows naught

*fourth movement*

. . . "grasshopper," xaolín master
whispered thunder, "when in
search for epiphany in aztlán,
make sure u leave some stones
unturned. these may be radioactive
make heads roll and fall out
when they broadcast about others
what they emanate themselves."


*ZAZ !!!!*

## culebra

las faldas de mexicali
trafican cilantro
orégano y limonadas
chimichangas cachanillas
nescafé y delicados sin filtro
tecates con sal y tequila chasers
menudo, conexiones con el centro y tranzas
con el d.f., san felipe camarones y política
norteña aunque guayabereando
desiertos de caribes
humedades
con todo
y sus platanares
los dátiles y las uvas
no dejan de hacer sangría
la noche huele a matadero
la sangre de toro
se bebe caliente
somoza ha muerto
bayoneteado, fusilado a trizas
con bazookas y metrallas automáticas
al sha se lo llevó el veneno de su bilis
arrogante mientras kissinger mantiene sus
diarios diplomáticos
zorreando más que rommel en el desierto
de madison y wall street
el vello de oro
todavía
danza con el toro
no hay capa, escudero o picador
con lanza que plante daga
al cerebellum
trans
nacional

rombos
círculos an
gulares y metá
foras simé tricas
dando movi miento y
medi da toda vía al
arch i tect, tecto y arquí
medes el vagabundo o sci pri ón
el afri can o la pala bra no
en tierra más bien colo ca
con tiene la sub stancia
cer e bral de ne uronas
únicas y flor e
cientes a romas
per fumes
a dole
scents

jazz i
ficando pel
daños arch e
o lógicos slabs up
on slabs epi taph
not ions a bout death
i la capa cid a de
ser im per ece de roca
si in mortal sin em bargo
carnal hue sudo y circu latorio
meta bólico re lámp a go lu min oso
de e ner gía ovular cáscara
blank i llos con sal sa ran
chera, era ché i 'ora
pos es lama lava
volcán y águila
es cameando
mon
soon

somoza
ha muerto
bayoneteado,
fusilado a trizas
con bazookas y metrallas
automáticas al sha se
lo llevó el veneno de su bilis
arrogante mientras kissinger
mantiene sus diarios diplomáticos
zorreando más que rommel en el desierto
de madison y wall street el vello
de oro todavía danza con el
toro no hay capa no hay
espada, escudero o
picador con lanza
que plante daga
al cerebellum
trans
nacional

feudo
valle de
imperiales tunas
latifundistas pistas
y tecnología guerrera
voladora brawley y los
cuarenta cadabras de alibaba
babeando cosechas de capataces
enganches coyoteros y pollos en
jaula de oro plateando gallos sudando
sangre con encapuchadas momias
y vampiros que no conocen
la joda, el sol, ni las
aceitunas, mucho
menos el nopalito
el ocote, no
se diga el
armadillo

cross
the desert
dusk que se
hundía sandía
peak pronosticaba
luna llena la rosa
ansiosa, lucía sus negros
ojos obsidianados en el peyote
del amanecer en manzanar
almacén y hogar de fuego lava
hortaliza matutina y dos
cadencias acopladas al adobe
y a la viga cenzontle
del crepúsculo del
río bravo y la
poda de canabis
vespertina
luna

las
faldas de
mexicali tra
fican cilantro
orégano y limonadas
chimichangas cachanillas
nescafé y delicados sin filtro
tecates con sal y tequila chasers
menudo, el centro connections y tranzas
con el d. f., san felipe camarones
y política norteña a'nque guayabereando
desiertos de caribes humedades con
todo y sus platanares los dátiles
y las uvas no dejan de
hacer sangría, la
noche huele a
matadero, la
sangre de toro
se bebe ca
liente

cien
pies bien
planteados
en la milpa
acojinada de la
alfombra espacial
de bombarderos nocturnos
los platillos voladores todavía
no aterrizan pues el maya
itzae se ha olvidado aun lacandón
y chontal hamaquean sin conocer
el rumbo que tomaron los
desaparecidos maestros
en el amanecer de
los carrizales águilas
vela y compás
misioneros
panalean
árboles

una
abeja me
mordió el
pulgar derecho
mas traiba tripas
largas, el aguijón flor
marchitaba sobre la huella
mientras la tijerilla rondaba
la mesa caoba dura quebraba la
dentadura de cualquier termita vagabunda
siempre y cuando que los gatos no garraran
su correteo nocturno ni las pezuñas
perrunas aplastaran su reconocimiento
as faltado en ceviches eslabones
perdidos en el esplendor
gracioso de las codornices
cazando grillos
y mariposas
encapullando
sueños

un
socio,
mentado
chester pataleaba
piedras, su home run
era el changarro de dillon
en dodge city chester tocaba
claves con el muslo de su pierna
en el porche de cualquier comercio
la kitty, gatita cantinera del main
hall cantaba y bailaba para calmar
cualquier brawl, el chester la
acompañaba con su waltz
para así cerrar
pues disney ya
había sacado a
su tinker bell
y su never
never
land

pero
no se lo llevó
el obispo con su
dogma, fe o milicia
la malició temprano y
se enamoró de la vela, el
pan y el vino la luz, la luna
el ocaso y el monte, en felino se
convirtió y sin querer y sin temerlo
empezó a merodear, a acechar, a
cazar sin rumbo conociendo las
veredas cascabeleando águilas
digiriendo cabras y
chupando flor de
maguey de puma a
colibrí papaloteó
teo papalo
o me
voló

pro
blemas te
nía con sus
loga ritmos con
gas base i quinto
cuqueando chicharra
veraniega playas marea
lunarena i grunions matu
tinos meseros de billares cál
culos angulares y bolea dos calcos
en oda dos en el zoquete de la
milpa mecanizada con diego
pro gramado en computadora
danzante, más allá de la
ceniza ocotera de
la nube roja roquiza
montañesca y
encañonada
con en dia
bladas
vere
das

cobbler
i calles
empedradas
tirando patín con
chanclas euzkadi, hua
raches micho a canos
pirelliando hules i quemando
huelgas ejidatarias amache tea das
en chiapas blokeando puentes con
garrafones de agüecaña, limones
naranjas i jaranas yuca te cas
guayabeando bombas retóricas
mientras el pri disquea
con mismaloya i
sus arcos sin
flecha
hecha

le
vita
zion
es han reta
do al viento y
cada uno de los
cinco soles quetzaleando
en venezuela temblores
que hoy aquejan guate mala
las cavernas de oro negro ora
culan la cobra del caribe isleando
palmas cocoteras y aceite puro y
puros, puros tabacos, café, azúcar
chicle y goma, resinas faenas
sin toro, bana ne ando la
selva sin ser devorado
por la bureau
cracia ni
la de men
cia

## academia

la academia babilónica
la de los laberintos abandonados
la de los panfletos revolucionarios
la de los profesores boticarios
la de los estudiantes vagabundos
    en un mundo que sólo
tiene lenguas para los iniciados
    en la retórica hueca
flautas gimen
    lo que en las aulas queja
así la ciencia
    se hace vieja
y la sabiduría caduca en las paredes
    de baños segregados

## there will b no bullfights this fall

hummingbirds suckle
today, i mean, there b
no clouds, one rose blooms
red pink and swallows drink
again our sweat, the pool b still
the learning has begun
honey bursts and trickles
out magnolia pistils
man today walking
old ancient begging
for alms proud face
cuauhnáhuac proud
and hungry, no family
no kin, a cot, tobacco
some squash, chile
maize tortillas
some beans and little hope
slow change crawling
revolutionary rhetoric rattles
in tenoxtitlán
. . . another mexican!
        . . . so be it!
reaganitis prevails
pyramidically a mummy
wails for a worthy
burial place
medically, in germany
sour reagan means
acid rain
a song reverberates
however, my ear
connects spinal
column revertebrates
the sound of it all

obsidian eyed
uranian smile
perfect writ
a habeas love
thy corpus, i?
u, talking to me?
grüss gott!!
in embracing kiss
been mirrored
eyes filled
with love, witnesses
these and those
sheets, humid yes
we have loved in
our red dawns
your blushing
cheekbones radiating
emanating peace
teeth have caressed
left shoulder now turned
between dark breasts, lies
left arm, humid up
'gainst ardor hot
vertical lips pulsate
between entwined pubis
legs laced dreaming
with our thighs
flesh has awakened
dawn, again, yes
world, thee, again
germersheim or phoenix
departing now, departing
now to bremen or león
below thee, northern star
the sun above us
below thee, rainbow glow
guiding light cross

asphalted smiles
somebody, some body
bee gerbil song
being born bell
tolling, clanging "zur"
the morn in bremen
sparks half moon train
to frankfurt people
exquisite smiles
throb a heartful
"we don't need mummies"
last i heart in deutschland
in tollán, mist returns
strolling down, up
tula giants
womankind, person
choice ankle foot
countenance full of mind
lost i, she fine featured
cheekbone kiss
mouth, waist, moon breasted
sigh, interlaced teotihuacán
thighs quivering
huracanes being
born thunder
words sparse
lips, all six wet
yes, life b choice
and so love b
vertical smiles
rain, yes tepoztlán i long still for thee
raza, u b
and i with u
there, where ce ácatl topiltzín
quetzalcoatl dialogued
with hummingbirds and
butterflies, papalotl

dew, dissipation
concatenation flapping
wings in guanajuato
here, dogs rule
seven to one
they outnumber humans
cats don't count though
siamese or otherwise
there b many more eyes
sparkles, dreams of survival
mummies remain mummies
and mute, wish ronnie
was here to see his fate
through alley streets
and "the crisis" his economy
has wrought, a plague
and, and, and, and
an old shoeless man spoke
to me of his old cacique feathers
lost, bygone with the exodus
of the villages youth searching
for work, rock'n, rock'n
rock'n'roll and hope
infrahuman powers here
in this colonial cloister hover
we are protected
golden carp can't touch one
the new mexico mondragones
should visit guanajuato:
dew drawn, the lines
at the tortillería
nahuales smiling
the pulque quilted
sierra waiting
. . . there will b
no bullfights this fall
in amerindia

## no habrá corridas este otoño

los colibríes se amamantan
hoy, digo, no hay nubes
una rosa florea roja roseada
y las golondrinas beben
otra vez nuestro sudor
el estanque inmóvil
el aprendizaje ha comenzado
la miel explota y se derrama
fuera de los pistilos de magnolia
un hombre, hoy, caminando
anciano antiguo pidiendo limosna
rostro enjuto de orgullo
orgullo cuauhnahuacense
hambriento, sin familia
ni parientes, un petate
tabaco, poco de calabaza
poco chile y tortillas
de maíz, unos frijoles
y poco de esperanza
los cambios sociales se arrastran
la teórica revolucionaria
cascabelea en tenoxtitlán
. . . ¡otro mexicano!
       . . . ¡así sea!
la reaganitis prevalece
piramídicamente una momia
aulla por un sepulcro digno
médicamente, en alemania
sour reagan quiere decir
lluvia ácida, envenenada
una canción reverbera
sin embargo, mi oído
conecta con la espina
dorsal que revertebrea

el eco del todo que murmura
ojos obsidianados
sonrisa uránica
escrito perfecto
un hábeas, amo
yo, vuestro corpus?
tú, me hablas, a mí?
grüss gott!!
en abrazador beso
me he reflejado
ojos llenos de cariño
vivificando estas
y aquellas sábanas
húmedas, sí
hemos amado
gozado nuestros
rojos amaneceres
tus ruborosos
pómulos radiando
emanando serenamente
lenguacariciando hombro
izquierdo, clavícula, ahora
entre morenos senos, palma
izquierda, húmeda arriba yace
entre ardientes labios verticales
pulsando, entrelazado pubis
piernas, muslos soñando
carnalmente hemos despertado
el amanecer, otra vez, sí!
mundo, vosotros, otra vez
germersheim o phoenix
partiendo ahora, partiendo
ahora a bremen o león
bajo vos, estrella del norte
el sol sobre nosotros
bajo vos, incandescencia arco iris
guiadora luz a través

de sonrisas asfaltadas
alguien, alguna persona
es canto de jerbo naciente
la campana repica
llamando "zur"
al amanecer en bremen
chispea el tren de media luna
la gente de frankfurt
de exquisitas sonrisas
palpita corazones satisfechos
"no necesitamos momias"
lo último que oí en deutschland
en tollán, el rocío regresa
paseando por doquier
gigantes en tula
hembra, mujer, persona
planta, pie, tobillo único
elegante porte felino
yo pierdo, ella fina
beso pómulo, boca, cadera
pezones lunares, suspiro
entrelazados, teotihuacán
muslos telúricos
los huracanes revuélcanse
bajo el trueno
el de las pocas palabras
labios, los seis
empapados, sí
la vida propone
tanto como el amor
sonríe verticalmente
llueve, sí
tepoztlán añórote
aún raza vos eres
y yo contigo allí
donde ce ácatl topiltzín
quetzalcoatl dialogaba

con las chuparosas
y las mariposas
aleteando concatenadas
en guanajuato
donde los perros reinan
siete a uno sobre
los humanos
los gatos no cuentan
siameses or lo que fueran
sobran los ojos chispeantes
soñando sobrevivencia
las momias serán momias
y mudas, quisiera que ronnie
estuviera aquí para ver
su sino por los callejones
y la "crisis" que su economía
ha fraguado, una peste
un hombre descalzo me habló
de sus antiguos amuletos de cacique
perdidos, olvidados en el éxodo
de la juventud pueblerina
en busca de trabajo por
los centros urbanos rockeando
rocanrolleando esperanzas
abrigando poderes, fe
infrahumanos aquí
en este claustro colonial
suspendidos en la atmósfera
la carpa dorada no nos puede tocar
estamos protegidos de diluvios
los mondragones de nuevo méxico
deberían visitar guanajuato
en las colas de la tortillería
se dibuja el rocío del ocaso
los naguales sonrientes
en espera la sierra
matizada de magueyes pulques

serenos los maracames
. . . no, este otoño no habrá corridas
no habrá corridas de toros este otoño
en amerindia

## squirrel

there b no
easy chair
in this here
country what
i call bomb
they call
a fair
if there ever
b life in tree
i call air
have no rhythm
have no rhyme
no rock
no stone
have heart
have people
b not much
to hawk, bald
eagle naught
someone rise
beyond storm
thy steeple
love not any one
meaningless
treasure persons
cross the mire
too much toilet
paper in the fire
stink like skunk
confucius say
carp out cooking
off thy nile
b no river
russian blast

starve not
sense sanity
clarity, no jelly bean
tonight, perhaps
a light out thy cave
pyramid survive
barfull lawyers
and writs for
the live, habeas
corpus fit
to behive
honey, hide the powder
on thy third eye
forehead

## cabezeando

cabezeando con la bruma
con la cuerda colora
que imagina culebras
noches sonoras
reverberando amaneceres
trabajos, labores
liberadas en su música
labrada en el espacio
tiempo medido
suspiro trazado
con pauta i con güiro
con grillos huraños
hurón cavernero
en tierra de hormigas
praderas carecen búfalos
carecen quetzal
i ríos limpios
aun las cucarachas
sufren las redadas
y raid conspira
con el d.d.t./i.t.t.
detente,
detente
ya tenemos neutron bombs

## tarrega

tarrega plucking
trickling thoughts
spraying tears
laughter bursting
edges overflowing
winging lava reefs
life is but a chord
music has bewitched
my soul brewing
dreams i b u are
your womb
the only clearing
through this garlic
woodland of melody
snow crisp above
the cradle moon
the morn flowers
feather by feather
smiles melt our
adolescent years
vinegar and salt
crown each other's
flesh drenched
cemetery angry
at the haughty

## me hablas

ya te lo dije ayer
que la falta
de tu tez
niega a mi soledad refugio
y mi pensamiento escapa
me hablas al oído
la humedad de tus labios
los verticales
cruzados sobre mi muslo
y tus palabras timbran
terremotos
acoge, acoge mi lluvia

# thy

thy dark ages
found your halls
filled with thee
gloss of flagellated
selves looking for,
thru a glass
darklee albert
bert and rob
no bobby, gun
present, police
thy purple wine
i sweat and re
member clearly
wesson forty-five
sunny daydream
maybe u have and
a colt thirty-eight
return, relocate
the seventh
seal play chess
past the checkers
and the pockets
full of blood
remain
the one that asks
concrete questions
treasure the
company and
the center with
or without
    feathers
thru obsidian
    see the light

## door windows

door windows
betray black phone
weighing scale
ushers astrological
charts and fortunes
blond dogs guard
the fellowship
the snails crawl
on the mirror
asphalt rooted
chinese elms
line the avenue
ink spills red
as oil hovers gray
every one b
careful now
not to cheat
the dusk from
its crimson

## candle twirl two

candle twirl two
pillows abound
kiss the dawn's
labia love melting
full of juices
entwined thighs
eyes sparkle
sharp on middle
foreheads sweat
sweet dreams
fleeting space
moments, truth
rama bull's head
rolls bleeding
sacrifice into
the pond of roses
the flame is still
the blossom open
the staff erect

# raging

raging rain rattles gutters
condominiums sway
ocean spray rustles
frogs croak spring blossoming
a dynasty is anew yin and yang

**no**

no conozco tinta
   que pinte bien tu hermosura
ante ti, el silencio vale
   y aun con verbo
no hay cura
   temo de ti
enamorarme. Pueblo
en el fragor de la lucha
como la trucha del mar
solo en río arriba
   doy luz
no es muy tarde
   si Dios hay
goza el conflicto
   pues en las clases
se da
   el cristal que Lo refleja

## bartolo's kuilmas

u remember, tomás?
smile, source
power, stalk
column, spinal?
. . . no, pos sí!
u remember, tomás?
wine, grape
thought, treasure
heart, dice?
. . . no, pos sí!
u remember, tomás?
rosarito lobster
awe, brilliance
impeccable self?
. . . no, pos sí!
u remember, tomás?
the paper poet's dawn?
the sand dunes
the coast?
. . . no, pos sí!
bent back sweat
shoulders, knees
calloused hands?
. . . no, pos sí!
i remember u,
tomás rivera
¿te acuerdas
de tu flor, tu canto
de tu llanto, tu mesquite
de tu paz, de tu armadillo?
. . . no, pos sí!
¿te acuerdas, rivera
de las cuerdas, de la lira
del bajo sexto, del acordeón

de las barras, de la chancla?
. . . no, pos sí!
¿te acuerdas, rivera
de las olas, las veredas
de las estrellas, las rocas
de la espuma, del ocelote!?
¿te acuerdas, rivera
del mar, del océano
del río, del valle
de la lucha, de la raza?
. . . no, pos sí!
¿te acuerdas, rivera?
. . . no, pos sí, ¿cómo no?
remember, tomás?
stark smile, yes
pleased with life
no complaints
. . . sí, pos no!
i remember tomás
telling him, even
that angry hearts throb
that "greens" treasure
. . . sí, pos no! no bombs!
i remember tomás
he say to me "hail
. . . believe in no führer!
b yourself, suffer not!"
. . . sí, pos no!
i remember tomás
he say "size b
a measure from the head
to the sky, lest it b
to the dust 'n' dirt"
. . . sí, pos no!
i remember tomás
yes
i remember your joy

tomás
me acuerdo, rivera
de tus ojos certeros
de tu palabra breve
de tu aura y obra
. . . sí, pos no!
me decías cuando
cuestionaba yo tanto
y con causa me rebelaba
. . . sí, pos no!
me decías "¡lucha
no te dejes, ni apendejes
sigue tu vereda!"
me acuerdo, rivera
que tú te acordabas
que tú amabas
que tú laborabas
que tú luchabas
me acuerdo, rivera
¿me olvido . . . ?
. . . sí, pos no!
¿cómo sacarte de mi alma?
"¡sácate la daga!"
me dijiste alguna vez
contestándote yo dije
" 'ta bien, dejemos
que'l tío sam
nos dé posada . . ."
". . . sí, pos no,
mejor a maría y a josé
¡pos en este mundo
tiene uno que andar
con 'mula'!"
con sonrisa replicaste,
rivera
te pregunté entonces,
tomás

que si la libertad valía,
que si la autodeterminación,
la nuestra, que si américa era
un solo continente
que si lograríamos ser
nosotros mismos
que si nuestra palabra
cruzaría el tiempo,
el espacio, las fronteras,
las galaxias, que si seríamos
al fin, uno, un solo pueblo
una sola tierra
y tú dijiste
". . . sí, pos claro
. . . no, pos desde luego
. . . sí, por supuesto
no pos . . . sin lugar a dudas"
. . . claro, tomás rivera, claro
¡no, no has desaparecido!
¡sí, sí estás presente!
esta daga se queda . . .
esta espina no daña . . .
esta flor no perece . . .
este canto no calla . . .
este canto no calla . . .
. . . este canto no calla

## filipinas

wait to hold u me zaz hola qué tal
equis children we are u and me just
world cruise balloon day evening
give life write we b being born
not busy dying blossoming stalk
do make a better, badder, more
awesome dewflower bullet cook
brother, sister, compañera, kababayan
trailsome road b pebbled rose
above, below, right, left, center beauty
wonder inquire heart mind love passion
qué tal zaz hola u me too hold wait
river deep pluck cry, die not, smile
honky tonk weary touch such well
bigsword dagger hara-kiri naught
dragons wail well above dinosaurs
white lite at nite b not brite
left us, us, nosotros
i ke uvas Corazón
solitude prevails
in the absence of Aquino
beasts b mortal, hosts art minotaur
this labyrinth i understand inside
zaz hola qué tal wait to hold u me

**mi vida**

mi vida
un libro abierto
donde las letras escurren
cucarachas en invierno
  buscando calor
entre tazas de café rancio
  o bien
hojas caídas
que en el otoño fertilizan
la tierra plagiada de burrócratas
alacranes, ensilabados en sus "memos"
buscando manera impune con
cual acallar mi voz, mi hoz
¡ . . . son tus algas, dijo el otro
    y aquí yo te monto potro . . . !

## ga yo ga

on the azotea
sitting by the barking multitude of dogs
howling to a guanajuato dusked full moon
my heart is at peace
the roar of wheels
and bolts and the hammering of stone
somehow this colibrí fluttering
war against the aguacate tree
plucking the nectar off,
succulent orbs of light
streaming up its beakneedle
make one a bell clanging
for another evening
san francisco or san diego mass
candles are lit
the calm finally embraces
the chisel is put away
the slabs lie about the street
the sancudo hunts, sun resting

## hijos

logo in ritmo
día lleno de norma
chale, nel . . . ¿polonia?
minería de carbones
núcleo la nucleación
lo nuclear i su fisión
¿fición, ficción? . . . ¡fisión!
imperativa fusión nuclear
los desechos atómicos son
indeseables, intolerables
insoportables desechos
imperecederos
ajos, ojos

## notice, not ice
### cooperate, or coop & rate

notice, notice, notice, not ice, notice, notice
this planet is for lovemaking and sexual peace
u seek to b understood yet give no understanding
no returns, give sometimes or care naught
and watch home turn to a dump, a junk yard
owls to hoot u thru murky moongloom darkness
sow frustration reap anger and eat dungheaps
of children's wrath and your mate's alienation
will grow thorns to crown another sacrifice in
vain in vanity into vampires turn the youth
suck the blood dry from the bone of contention
contempt and incontinenced self-righteousness
can drag a faithful dog to rabid and
distempered wails at the center of a storm
where dishes, clothes and faces unclean
brew stench and misery and rust to dust
notice, notice, not ice not ice, notice, notice
after yourself clean up your self-serving act
before u become the judge of others learn to give
selflessly with a smirk meet your foe worry not
act with mercy unafraid and without arrogance b
loved.

## back in califas

last i heard
humphrey the whale
came up river
the Sacramento
to challenge "the duke"
and his elephant head
while bradley and
desmond tutu
divest
and readily reinvest
their hearts
and their minds
meanwhile, sandinista
self-determinant deseos
remind the world
that "the debt"
is not only
**not payable**
**but not**
**collectable**
**either**

# cluster

monarch butterflies cluster on eucalyptus trees, in twos, in clans reagan drowns in the stupor of credible deniability, the russians wait un calorcito interno busca la otredad, the killing, the madness must stop building a nest, twig by twig, spit and mud, feathering, winging it un código interno qué dice tú y yo, nosotros o nadie o nada or no body ballenas grises migrating to Baja, their fate to mate, to survive, to b returning al estrecho de Bering, to frolic, to dive deep, to sea, yes! dawn kissing stars away, sun rising, dew settling ... Califas ... i ke! dusk embracing wild orchids with its crimson mist, war ... war ... war what is war good for? nothing! absolute business! absolute profit! wet brown earth sprouting oak strength branches off trunk leaves nicaraguan children wishing well to their northamerican counterparts contrapartes childless, humorless, futureless, lifeless, less bomb, many a songwail has been heard and helicopters crashed in the jungle ho chi minh turns his grave unearthed by koranic mullas dog matized rabid and equivocated christians and muslims miss the point. dogma kills, faith blinds. desire pangs. war, what it is, is good, damn good business profit. accumulation. wealth material in few bellies, cast at our cost wicked. metamorphosed beyond human recognition, revelation, revolution? there b no more space for deceit, pointmen and armsdealers breathe hollow dust barrels of steel carry out death past our future mind naught present hunger ... ignorance ... disease ... OUR hunger, OUR ignorance, OUR disease! do WE ALL matter? are WE, ALL here? ¿somos o no somos? ¿estamos o no? ayatollah y ronnie no saben qué, ni cómo, ni cuándo, ni dónde, ni nada! hummingbirds suckle and cormorants dive deep, deer examine, doe taste. roses bloom on the cancerous polyps of warmongers. sick soldiers ooze ...

following orders not ordered, fighting wars not declared,
wallow, deep nica, nica, nica . . . compa NICARAGUA
lives past all western and

eastern mire . . .

YES! I KE!

# friday today

friday today father matters, three vultures feasting on a doe gathering plucking away her life bleeding coyotes watching close by butterflies wondering and hovering yet avoiding carnage hummingbirds flutter fully aware that war b destruction of the human spirit and the cactus flower blooms roses to roses thorns ashes to ashes death is the hunter and only one heart prevails amidst the hunger that tears love b the answer hope b the calling faith the discipline b one to do what has to b done in passion with unbending intent treasure the sparkle of an eye and the toothful smile of peace yes this morning children waited for thirteen pointed deer to get them through the fog all the way to the center of becoming teachers wait for their arrival early safe sane healthy protected and smiling we joined a pack of coyotes, the plot remained victory one can only imagine moonful reflections mother searching a face out in the midst and the mist of father adorns petals and warms stalks, corn rises to feed the people and he works beauty that it may surround thee precious ones the rainbow past the chaos and the mire reasoning wallow blind man and woman miss each other through her turn to walk about search-ing for her own leads return one to palms swaying to the origin fountains flow freely warm in the milky way acceptance welcomes with a hug and arms b cast into plows earth longs for within wet and wanting stuff bel-lies bloat and frowns abound were we just to b two pleased with the glow of happy children learning that castles need not house or incarcerate a simple sincere innocent soul in love in life on earth

## yo, gracias a dios

yo, gracias a dios no sé nada de nada de algo me pregun-
tan y yo pues respondo las algas nos han de dar la vida
algún día lleno, nublado pero yo qué sé pequeño hombre enamorado de una sola mujer que pues vale más
que su peso en oro la plata brilla como aquella piedra
llamada alexandrina que aquí pocos pencos conocen y yo
pos apenas sé nadar y no me ahogo en las pendejadas de
estos vellos púbicos si yo sé amar es porque la vida vale
más que un toro sin capa y sin picador las azucenas y las,
sí, las rosas y los pequeños magueyes florecen con las
buganvillas que adornan sus palmas mientras mis pies
pisan la arena no hay tiburones que cosechen mis plan-
tas pues toninas me protegen hay enanos que guardan
sus greñas largas para acometer hongos que no conocen
que sin embargo han de vengar sus impúdicas muecas
¿a poco nomás porque ella sirve y él que la quiere, tiene
derecho a decir yo tiré más ochos que los que raquean?
algunos de nuestros hermanos han perecido por seme-
jantes afrentas yo todavía atesoro las flores, las lágrimas
de nuestros bebos las hojas de cualquier árbol que gima;
¡tengo sed! el amor no es cosa del otro mundo ni magia
ni cosa maravillosa es solamente la única energía que
vale y que dura y dura y dura y se mantiene contenta y
pues yo qué sé pequeño lleno de ojos y sonrisas quisiera
yo saber hablar, conocer la palabra que nos reúna y nos
recuerde lo mejor de nosotros, son otros los que desvían
esta ofrenda pues en realidad somos pocos los que
hablamos y escribimos in glyph las estrellas sobre tarra-
gona auguran los morros, las olas los pelícanos se clavan
sobre las olas en la playa de almejas villa, dónde estás
cuando busco a zapata, merxe!

## a bank

for the flemings in oakland, rick & bee


a bank held its tongue while man attempted dialogue
unmoved
he, shoeless cross the winter night winds of a
berkeley night
unmoved
razor sharp stone tongues rattled black obsidian
past tonight's
full moon
i have nothing to say
the students speak for themselves, it is dawn and
dawn in california
b red, she
a narrative, a story to tell beyond the mire of
reaganitis inflamed
tonight i smirk and celebrate
defeat contra aid, aids be enough to handle at home
don't get me wrong
or worse, do not get me right. i do give a hoot, i
care though i
b naught enough owl
lost i in the wilderness of asphalt funding, yet i
b brought back
to us, to we, to b
one
two
do
what
has two
b
done
the bank not unlike jericho reminded the monologue
to speak
in numbers

in code correct
walled in process
programmed progress prayer chant
beat palestinians at the horse races get a jockey
scholar ride
lottery, bingo, alas, eureka, aleluya, vote? for
whom? what for?
rainbow be enough?
is jackson a preacher man who tells it like it is?
or was j.c. crucified?
what it is, is what it does!

## guadalupanas

huracán songs
    trickle up sparkles
flaming into wealth
    light showering mirrors
       serpent uraxan
feathered cloud thunder
    thunder clapped
thunder to dance
    circle round people
thunder to dance
withinwithout
    heartstruggle builds
and the revolt is imminent
    huracán, uraxan pueblo
bluegreen rain fall
    in the dawnmist
    blue green rain rain
for the pawnfist
      now it can see
can cut the strings
    silklaced these monkeys
genuflect to gorillas
    the hostmaterial pleasure
rises with the standard
    of behaviormodification
lobotomies abound and
    so do fences, adobewalls
fix cactus curtains
there b no tunas
no spiderweaving
    crowns wallow wingless
past all these torrents
    ashes turn
cockroaches

there b no raid to stop
the current
the river, the flux
   in solitude we drink
we drink our blood
   we sacrificed our
adolescent seeds
   guadalupanas
bear guns today
it's sweeter that way
. . . tú sabes

## Xaman say

Xaman say stop playing with chains they may enslave u
the world invites the letting go of bondage kneel naught
stand erect and stare at the dawn naked unafraid all
giving surrender power cast in armor and discover the
pearl within the shell that u thought guarded u a dia-
mond awaits the pressure of gravity of earth holy
mother sun father wind mother water carbon b necessary lest brother tree and sister flower choke, b us the
ones to populate the mountains with seed and the val-
leys gulleys and deserts even with cactus that pulque
may flow again pulsating to the radiation of a benign
light heat and drought u know the glaciers are melting
and capturing the songs of whales though sharks
abound pelicans call out the dolphin and the ants and
the bees gather men and women will live, will survive
our own cruelty greed and blindness hummingbirds
will bring the pollens into our hearts and all phobias
will perish and the morning star will give birth to sacred
twins again a tree of life shall blossom and wisdom shall
dance upon the dew as clouds gather in dialogue fear is
the enemy and then clarity may deceive our nuclear dis-
coveries yet power will surrender to the magma that
we'll breathe past the military nightmares of the igno-
rant and blind Xaman say wipe out catch a great big
turtle and learn to walk on water measure the stars'
motion and understand once and for all that our
collective consciousness constitutes the architect and the
architecture we are tonal we are nahual we are one, one
is us, yes.

**faseal**

urbanrenewal, así, in one word, the character of the
barrio was to b or not to b, ser or no ser . . . the barrio was
to b transformed into the brave new world of behavior
modification that the terminators in city hall had con-
cocted as a solution to their fear and ignorance because
that is what it was. fear, what to do with these mexicans.
i mean the blacks had been enough of a problem and the
mexicans had acquiesced right after the zoot suit riots of
the forties but their heirs had sprouted right up in a
mean way because this time around they were not at a
loss for a cause. no señor, this time there was this thing
called chicano movement brewing locally just as ho chi
minh was drafting his own, to cast off the european
invasion and cut the new opium wars off at the pass
with class struggle. the strategy seemed to be holy,
wouldn't u know it! cut the barrios in half or quarter
them colonial style with an asphalt horse, nevermind
troy or helen fact is our barrios like everything else in
the corporateman's world were to b dissected, analyzed,
and synthesized into a profitable protean manifestation
of an appropriately appropriable anomic and anemic
strata of, in their mind, the rabble at the cross progress
side road to nowhere they, citystepfathers, figured for
the dwellers of caquita shores known by that name only
by the homeboys in "la logan" initiated into the art of
placa spraying the wall and marking turf with an urban
tattoo. ¡y ke! cuatro milpas survived eventhough the
prices went up. a bowl of rice-beans-and-chile-colorado-
with-all-the-tortillas-u-or-i-could-eat was only one cora
or, as it were, twenty-five calcos or scents. the murales
were to come later as el queso got sandwiched into the
torta that our jalapenean movimiento got aged to fla-
vor, savor the illustrator and our image; nevermind the
carclub that later arrived humping asphalt down the

broken line that was designed to b a hi güey petrol station smack in the middle of thee, barrio-no-colon-ia, ia ya, ya basta con, con, don don don diego . . . ¿quo vadis?

## on the beach

on the beach chair i
he, thinking across the peaks
   slushing, joshing i
but not really, the snow
b as much his as the sun mine
   borges, said i
and he thought, jorgeluis
   of course, the hummingbird
sucks on
and the willow weeps
and dylan is bob
   even though thomas was
and is
   a good poet, he lived off
his agenda, while tomás
   has his hawk eye
   on the line
   the borderline, yes
the grand littleman
   él, comandante
   poeta de la sierra
   sandina tierra
i listen
"hablando se entiende
   la gente," true
so true. premise however
lawned on talking which
   implies a two-way arrow
shot
   put well, witty
did anybody listen. well
english is now the "official"
   language in california
mister, had to legislate it pal

a'nque the flow brook
cannot be adobed (from adobe
    building blocks that
    construct houses, applesheds
    and ovens).
in the southern west
or the western south
    as thou may play thy spool
weave cotton so
    hermano, compadre
uniformed parodies politik
    world is at hand
like a harpsichord
    only the melody waits
tom rhythms blues and crimsons
    light out cave
b weaponless
        i must tell this story
now. least house of lead
        and computers, pencil
ink sunset well
    bring the water up
worry not
suicide is no longer a personal
        choice
transnational bargaining chips
    chumps chump change
. . . ¿y nosotros qué? ¿voz otros qué?
    pos nada, nadan adán
papier-mâché, papel, paper
    pauper smash
has only bridges to sleep
        under
stated wealth and property
        rights
    white maidens writ
        título

árbol que vuela vela
    hamaca que conoce
el rock más antiguo
    mécese!
la democracia can only b
    in a kellogg's cereal
box prize
    lotería
malcolm x was the first
    víctima
kennedy and king got it
    as well, ni modo
el fascismo may have had
    more tentacles than
anyone ever imagined
    in germany
    in the u.s.a., tentáculos
since the hiroshima bomb
    and its banking
        pockets
this is not a critique
    in glyph
    or spinach
        olive oil
whaLE mEAT
    future shock chooses
pesticides, agent orange
and, well
    weALTH county
here i sit on pismo
    hills. libélulas
frolic and he writes memos
    funding cowards, no . . .
        misguided, hungry
lost militaristic egos, he goes
    seeding death
and they, unemployed

        unschooled
        follow powder contra
    the smell sweet
    the bullet swift
rooster burning there b no dawn
    fall choppin' lettuce. let us
col, cabbage, garbage haul out
        winter nears and the
    chinese masses will not starve
    he, duck sits, plucking
bleak
    pimple heads, tinkerbell
        b starwars
yet i . . .
        . . . high noon?
pistoled high plains
    drift, draft?
. . . wish popeye was here
        in the harbor full
moths  hover
    deceit and deception
presidential prerogatives prevail
        ronny is really peter pan
and nancy, wendy
    qaddafi, captain cook
and the usa never, neverland
        wonder how castro
fits in this story
    i personally think him
an ewok.
        . . . who needs fantasy,
sci fi or horror when
    the u.s. is enough?
. . . i know! i got it! the ussr
        anathema!

# chort fallin' blues

clintonicillin b dispensed from white house yet wilsonitis prevails preaching psalms for prisons in califas no
cure in sight yet for aids ignorance or racism thriving in
desastrelandia fraught by quakes and floods and fire-
storms and mudslides in malibu three feet high there b
no dinero for schools teachers or libraries let alone
librarians walking unemployment lines lengthening no
end in sight recession dipping down to short fallen
budgets buying border guard beef up as agent gets
acquitted in arizona for killing mexican sin documentos
looking for work no daily tortilla ready to b rolled con
chile pos tampoco hay arroz ni frijoles though an adobe
wall and cactus curtain rise aunque la pared de berlín y
la cortina de hierro cayeron and cuban tabaco y azúcar
are anatema in new age politically correct productos de-
seables vietnamese zinc and selenium may yet lift the
embargo against its borders but cuba's remain unspoken
on lips that can't b read enunciating free trade there
though we now do it with the rusos qué sura, no?
¿quién les entiende? . . . ni en su propia casa dijo ella
when she read about the ratón megabrain experimento
with electrodes enchufados to the hedonistic centers in
rats joyfully dying failing to provide themselves with
food drink and rest or partake of the luxury and abun-
dance served on the other side of their spacious cage
opting instead for the incessant pressing of pleasure
pedals perdiéndose pudriéndose placenteramente las
cárceles albergan adictos and the bancos profit from
mediatized sales of products unnecessary for wealth
wisdom or wellness scarce commodities in a market
where divorce drugs 'n' drive-bys plague family and
country también blacks killing blacks in south africa y
cualquier ghetto mexicans killing mexicans en cualquier
barrio including la madrepatria asians killing asians in

california and hong kong whites b killing whites in eastern europe and every low income hood in yankee-landia cupboards to coffins b common in sarajevo gun sales going up everywhere hunger ignorance injustice b imbedded institutionally calpulli time coming to méxico ejido warriors rising out zapatista ashes planting derechos indigenistas en chiapas y guatemala bleeds on amerindia clamors por un nuevo socialismo new rainbow yet to brighten earth's crust or the face of all children in its bosom la esperanza for a new day resides in the will of man and woman to say no to fear and greed and yes to love and miracles will happen if we struggle sing and salsa dijo ella letting go of fear serenely letting go of greed tranquilos saying yes to love y sus milagros struggle sing and salsa . . .

|    |        |           |       |      |   |          | vamo' |
|----|--------|-----------|-------|------|---|----------|-------|
| ya | pueblo | amerindio | vamo' | to'o | a | lucha'   | vamo' |
| ya | pueblo | del asia  | vamo' | to'o | a | libera'  | vamo' |
| ya | pueblo | europeo   | vamo' | to'o | a | lucha'   | vamo' |
| ya | pueblo | africano  | vamo' | to'o | a | libera'  | vamo' |
| ya | pueblo | arcoiri'  | vamo' | to'o | a | humaniza'|       |

. . . ¿que no?

. . . ¡que sí, chico! ¡que sí! ¡que sí!

## it has been said

it has been said that when
the poet misplaces sorrow
his song is lost, the vision ceases
hunger invades, hearts b
violent force and poverty abounds
southern children smile
northern powers stalk
resources, birthright and sweat
if they only knew that the only gold
to b swept in the "states"
lies plastered on the streets
. . . mashed chicklets
afterall, mexican

## mantra

wilsonitis is an ingrown
    epidemic
 in the heart of aztlán
187
 its pus